KT-219-611

C016495329

WITHDRAWN

Painfully British Haikus

MICHAEL JOSEPH
an imprint of
PENGUIN BOOKS

Painfully British Haikus

Dale Shaw

MICHAEL JOSEPH

UK | USA | Canada | Ireland | Australia
India | New Zealand | South Africa

Michael Joseph is part of the Penguin Random House group of companies
whose addresses can be found at global.penguinrandomhouse.com

Penguin
Random House
UK

First published 2019
001

Copyright © Dale Shaw, 2019

The moral right of the author has been asserted

Text Design by Francisca Monteiro
Set in ITC Legacy Serif
Printed in Great Britain by Clays Ltd, Elcograf S.p.A.

A CIP catalogue record for this book is available from the British Library

ISBN: 978-0-241-42974-7

www.greenpenguin.co.uk

MIX
Paper from
responsible sources
FSC® C018179

Penguin Random House is committed to a
sustainable future for our business, our readers
and our planet. This book is made from Forest
Stewardship Council® certified paper.

An Introduction

I have been asked to write AT LEAST five hundred words (MINIMUM) as a way of introducing this book, my book, of haikus concerning the British psyche or, in a way, the psyche of those residents that make up England, Wales, Scotland and Northern Ireland aka Britain or sometimes Great Britain or even the United Kingdom. And I have agreed to do this. Completely agreed. Without argument.

The *Oxford English Dictionary* defines a 'haiku' as 'a Japanese poem of seventeen syllables, in three lines of five, seven and five'. In the dictionary, it is next to the word 'haik' (a large outer wrap worn by people from North Africa', and 'hail' (pellets of frozen rain falling in showers from cumulonimbus clouds'). Three things which, I think you would have to agree, differ from each other greatly.

While a haik would probably come in quite handy if you were caught in a hail shower, a haiku probably wouldn't be that helpful. Unless it was a haiku of your own devising which (using seventeen syllables in three lines of five, seven and five) reminded you of what to do in a hail shower or, alternatively, where you could buy a nice haik.

Wow. Not even halfway yet. That's surprising. Very, very, very surprising.

So what is it about these Japanese poems of seventeen syllables, in three lines of five, seven and five that is so effective in illustrating the psyche of those residents that make up England, Wales, Scotland and Northern Ireland aka Britain or sometimes Great Britain or even the United Kingdom? That is an excellent question. A really, really excellent question.

For what is an Englishman? Or, for that matter, an English woman? Let alone a Welshman, Scotsman or Northern Irishman as well as a Welsh woman, Scots woman or Northern Irish lady? Well, to put it quite, quite simply, they are a resident, who happens to live in one of those four locations. And then there's the Channel Islands. Plus Gibraltar. And any number of overseas territories.

And thus, this makes them the perfect candidate for haiku which, as you will recall, is a Japanese poem of seventeen syllables, in three lines of five, seven and five as so perfectly defined by the *Oxford English Dictionary*, which printed its first edition, in Oxford, all the way back in 1884, when things such as Penny Farthings, large moustaches, cholera and hooped skirts were very popular.

And so, finally, in conclusion, what you hold, right now, in your hand or hands, is a joining together, or a combining if you will, or possibly a mixing, of these two fascinating occurrences. The classical form of the Japanese haiku (a poem of seventeen syllables, in three lines of five, seven and five) with the psyche, or character, of those residents, residing in England, Wales, Scotland and Northern Ireland plus any overseas territories.

I really hope you enjoy it. Really, really, really enjoy it.

For Daisy, again

Sausage utilized
As a makeshift barrier
Against breakfast beans

The Sellotape end
Unlocatable it seems
Christmas is cancelled

The sound of a splash
My Hobnob falls to pieces
My tea is sullied

Restaurant terror
Was that vintage wine I picked?
Not second cheapest?

Coming in to land
You'd rather hear the plane crash
Than hear mass applause

At the cinema
Eating starch in the darkness
Carpet sticks to feet

'Is this seat taken?'
'Oh no please do help yourself'
Said through gritted teeth

I don't mean to judge
But your leg tattoo display
Troubles me greatly

'Nice weather for ducks!'
Probably said many times
On the Titanic

A fox by the bins
Licking a Fray Bentos tin
It's not quite Springwatch

Morning ablutions
The toilet bowl is skidless
Today will be good

Christmas bin day fear
Turkey carcass smells pungent
Bin bags running low

Foreign hotel room
Your adaptor lies dormant
Why such a big plug?

It is last orders
But it's only half past ten
Where else is open?

'Is there anyone
Who objects to this wedding?'
All eyes turn to me

Dinner party guest
Has failed to bring us some wine
So put next to Clive

Your mother chimes in
'You won't feel the benefit'
The coat remains on

How is the weather?
A hurricane blows outside
'Looks a bit iffy'

Failed memory
Then pained capitulation
'How do you take it?'

Sinking sensation
It's a Facebook friend request
From your racist aunt

Every houseplant
Suffers a slow painful death
I am a monster

Repairman summoned
Appliance is on the fritz
Works when they arrive

The kitchen drawer
Blocked by a big spatula
Unfairness defined

This dog and my crotch
Are permanently conjoined
May have to marry

Back home for Christmas
By the 26th you think
'Who are these people?'

Full English breakfast
Tomatoes are eaten first
Get them out the way

A choice of swim trunks
Or novelty Santa pants
Laundry must dry soon

You can't help but think
A siren in the distance
Have they come for you?

A gurgle erupts
Must have been the kedgeree
This lift will suffer

The remote control
Is nine inches from my grasp
May as well be Mars

Try to change a plug
Will you be horribly charred
As you flick the switch?

Disproportionate
That is the anger you feel
At the scratchy towel

Wardrobe malfunction
Washing machine must be broke
Jeans are now too snug

'Sorry we missed you'
The card sits on the mat with
Insincerity

Twenty-five minutes?
For pizza delivery?
Can that be legal?

Loo roll diminished
Unravel the cardboard bit
And hope for the best

Why are books of stamps
So tiny and losable?
Fit them with a flare

Look, the sun is out!
Time for an al fresco lunch
With twelve thousand bees

Forget five a day
I have got it down to two
Walker's Squares and Lilt

'Please just go inside'
Aimed at your next-door neighbour
With telepathy

Keys left in the lock
A gas bill found in the fridge
Age is a prankster

Front seat, upper deck
Is there a greater pleasure?
Pretending to drive

Parallel parking
I've never felt more alive
As it's done in one

I fear that a bird
Has defecated on me
'It's good luck' says tit

No it's not a threat
Or sexy innuendo
'Can I top you up?'

'I'm me!' You bellow
As your computer denies
You even exist

A telephone call
The number has been withheld
Why not just stab me?

Nothing scarier
Public toilet cubicle
And the lid is down

A new adventure
As you flip the soiled latch
Vacant to engaged

Succumbed to sunburn
Skin the shade of a fresh weld
Savlonned to the sheets

'Piece of piss' you say
And try to leap a bollard
It does not end well

A long umbrella
Doubles as a decent lance
When necessary

In each other's way
The tango of the pavement
New nemesis made

Bunting indicates
Something fun is taking place
But nothing too fun

Bin bag has ruptured
Juice oozes onto slippers
Nearby pigeon laughs

Sickly car boot sale
Desperate smiles from vendors
Flogging body wash

There's a disc jockey
'Spinning' in this public house
Landlord is a dick

Litter drop witnessed
Picked up and deposited
By you with sarcasm

They have moved the plums
Supermarket trip sullied
Fruitless aisle search starts

Plastic bag handle
Strains under the weight of carbs
Will it make it home?

On the motorway
Bladder reaches breaking point
Between services

You're at the seaside
A seagull eyes your Magnum
You won't win that fight

Dog poo in a bag
Bag then left on the pavement
Why bag poo and go?

By the clock tower
Fat man with a hand-held fan
Confirms a heatwave

Caught short, pee by skip
Didn't spot the camera
Wait for the sirens

The queue has dissolved
Interloper squeezes in
Where's my cattle prod?

Charity shop wrath
Why are they charging so much
For charred dungarees?

The quiet carriage
A ringtone breaks the silence
Every sinew tensed

Some dismal bench plaques
Adorn all of this seating
I pick the least sad

The smokers outside
That's where the real party is
Bitterness chokes you

A phone number smeared
On a public toilet wall
Advertising counts

Discarded brown pants
Left by the side of the road
The tales you could tell

This garden centre
Has destroyed my will to live
Is there a bar here?

Man up a ladder
Cheery old-fashioned workman?
Or a crap burglar?

The fateful sentence
'Sorry we're out of the lamb'
While smug twat chews shank

Inevitable
Heavens suddenly open
Cagoule stowed elsewhere

Post office, queueing
Why do so many old men
Need so many stamps?

Fear at fishmongers
Will the fish man laugh at my
Paltry cod portion?

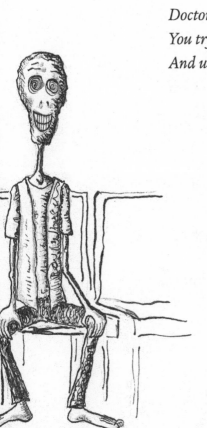

Doctor's waiting room
You try to assess who's next
And who's contagious

You mentally skim
Through your excuse Rolodex
Then approach your boss

Painful grin offered
Secret Santa's delivered
Charity shop soon

This country ramble
Has morphed into a death march
Is moss edible?

'Oh my giddy aunt'
Not a phrase you would expect
From your accountant

To really annoy
Your local grammar nazi
Spell pedants, pedant's

Why must I make tea
For co-workers I can't stand?
They deserve dryness

Seat free on the bus
You approach it gleefully
Then see why it's free

I honestly feel
This pedestrian crossing
Is haunted by dicks

Chugger in my path
I go the long way around
Guilt trip avoided

I have great hunger
Can I wait for my dinner?
Or will snacks derail?

Office Christmas do
Already disgraced yourself
Before buffet's out

Your tea has been made
But the milk has putrified
Proof there is no god

There's a hand dryer
There are also paper towels
You have made your choice

'Can I have a word?'
Is there a more chilling phrase
To hear your boss say?

You reach your front door
Desperate for the toilet
Keys are on your desk

Can I sponsor you
To just stay away from me
And not the fun run?

Leaving card on desk
True feelings must be suppressed
'Sad to see you go'

Why is my baguette
Sitting on a piece of slate?
Was it on the roof?

Sometimes I ponder
Is it me that's the problem?
No, it's the others

At the coffee shop
The hot barista shuns you
With your milky choice

'There's no I in team'
'But there's two in idiot'
Said under your breath

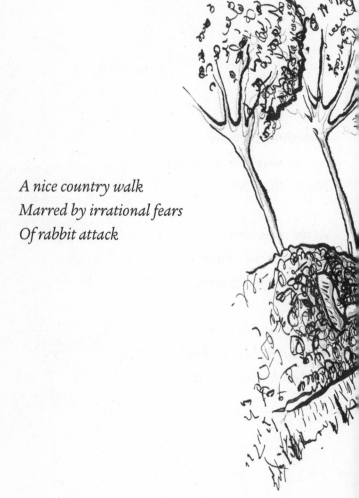

A nice country walk
Marred by irrational fears
Of rabbit attack

A sneeze in a lift
Will they all be offended
If I say 'Bless you'?

Painful hangover
I require something salty
And then something sweet

Novelty T-shirt
Are you being ironic?
Or are you just shit?

Smugness overload
Your remembered umbrella
As drizzle descends

Humiliation
Reply all to an email
With a misjudged gif

A door held open
No 'Thank you' is forthcoming
'You're welcome' you say

Sunstroke, braying kids
Cheap cider and tinnitus
I love festivals!

Wonder of snowfall
Too quickly transformed into
The bollocks of slush

Cone on a statue
They may as well just add them
At the sculpting stage

Powerpoint breaks down
You look helplessly around
At grinning faces

Your microwaved prawns
Are making a mockery
Of my desk-bound lunch

You approach the bar
But you already forgot
Your table number

Why are you calling?
That involves conversation
An email's silent

Browser history
Who knew that two simple words
Could cause such havoc

Exclamation marks
And the caps in your email
Lead to much sighing

A lightbulb moment
Why not make lightbulb fittings
All the bloody same

Doorbell is ringing
It is after ten o'clock
Cocoa is ruined

Why is a crumpet
Freshly out of the toaster
Hotter than magma?

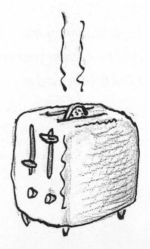

I have a ticket
So why do I feel such guilt?
Conductor looks on

At the rock concert
I enjoyed the first three songs
Now can I go home?

A quandary's offered
'In a mug or in a cup?'
Philosophical

Barbecue won't light
Lighter fluid suggested
Eyebrows soon vanish

And now it's raining
Why am I punished so much
For being outside?

Flap or not to flap?
The eternal debate flares
As a wasp intrudes

A lacklustre meal
'Is everything all right?'
'Oh delicious, thanks'

Child loose in the pub
Could not huff any harder
If I had asthma

Face full of drizzle
Shivering in a lay-by
Bank holiday fun

We must tidy up
Before the hotel maid comes
Though she's paid to clean

Lost in a strange town
You'd rather circle Lidl
Than ask directions

Back of a taxi
Eyes are fixed on the meter
With fierce disbelief

'I was having that'
But the same meal can't be picked
It's a commandment

It does feel as if
You're the lone one not coughing
In this cinema

Oh no. Time stands still
'I believe you're in my seat'
A shame shuffle starts

A breakfast buffet
A foreign toaster awaits
Bread soggy with sweat

'Does it come with chips?'
The waiter looks on appalled
You fake a nose bleed

Shouting very loud
I think I am understood
In a foreign land

Bag on a train seat
A special place in Hades
Is waiting for you

'Be my guest' you say
Proffering your bag of chips
And staring daggers

How many gin tins
Is decreed appropriate
For this train journey?

Awaiting your meal
'We were seated before them'
Tight-lipped stares commence

Panic envelops
Your ticket has migrated
Pocket to pocket

Gammon egg and chips
Why do I even bother
Eating other meals

Vandalized grit box
A squat yellow reminder
Of youthful hi-jinks

In an unknown town
Every passing car stares
It's as if they know

Autumn has arrived!
You playfully kick some leaves
Then spot the dog shit

Drunk and heading home
'What's the worst thing I can eat?'
You think to yourself

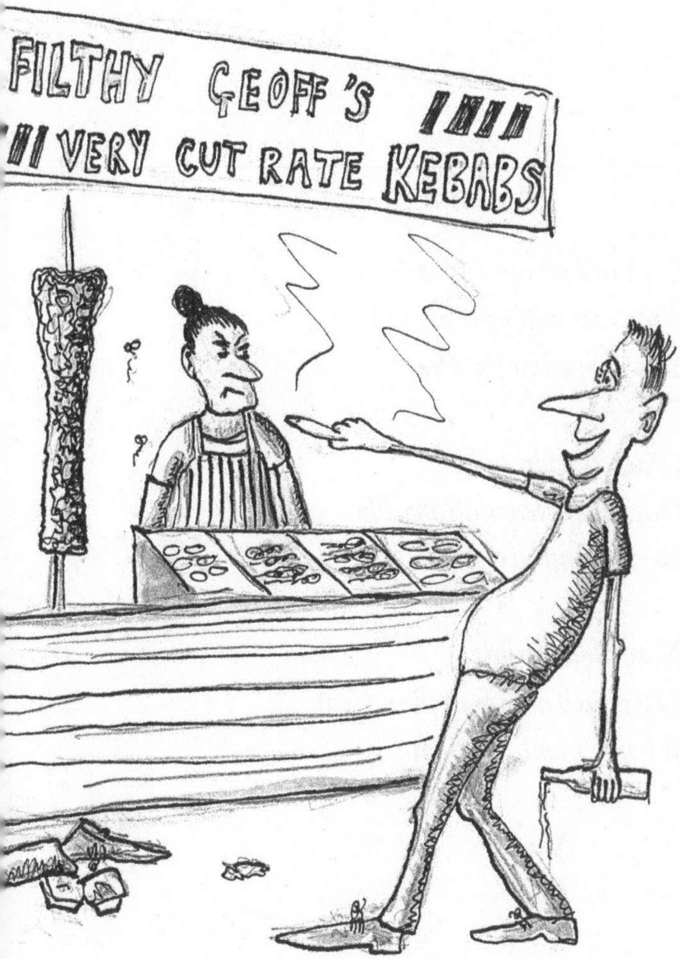
FILTHY GEOFF'S
VERY CUT RATE KEBABS

'Last orders now, please'
How can that possibly be?
You popped in for one

Coach station toilet
Has taken years off my life
So cold and so cruel

Never look inside
The pouch on an airplane seat
Where crumbs go to die

Rainy train window
Blurred image of a sad cow
Releasing a pat

Outdoor swimming pool
Can't let the cold water breach
Above my tit line

Sign says no smoking
But surely that man's smoking?
No, breathing badly

The pure tyranny
A complex sushi menu
'Just egg and chips, please'

Why are kebab shops
So well illuminated
To highlight my shame?

Enter hotel room
Check every cupboard door
Then put telly on

Baggage carousel
Jockeying for position
Where the bags shit out

Baffling car park
Look for man in a hi-viz vest
Bent ticket in hand

Ruined roast dinner
Why the hell is there sweetcorn
In amongst the peas?

'Tell me what you want!'
You scream out of the window
At the dawn chorus

On a British beach
Sunscreen not necessary
But a windbreak is

A rural airport
Vending machine offers treats
In a foreign way

On an aeroplane
Just because your seat reclines
Doesn't mean it must

Sleeping in a tent
Sweating in a sleeping bag
Slugs on your pillow

Volcanic anger
At the seeming injustice
Of the ham bap price

Ignored by barman
Despite my fierce eye contact
And desperate smile

Quick drink after work
Turns slightly more destructive
You wake in Swindon

Karaoke pain
Smiles melt away from faces
During your 'Jolene'

The check-in desk queue
Your big suitcase on the scale
The verdict awaits

Trying to express
Correct facial expressions
Baby's no looker

Bottle is brandished
'Would you like to try the wine?'
You sniff it of course

Shabby pantomime
Performer is in the aisle
Do not catch their eye

Bike on the pavement
Oh for the ability
To conjure punctures

A new year beckons
Exercise and diet planned
Love of Hobnob wins

In our lexicon
Are there three more chilling words?
Rail replacement bus

How can pick and mix
Be so much more expensive
Than top-grade cocaine?

My luggage contains
The same stuff that I left with
So why won't it fit?

The sight of a man
Wearing a bow tie gladly
Always unnerving

Ice cream or custard?
Now I know how Sophie felt
When she made her choice

'Can I use your loo?'
The words drift over the bar
Like a veiled threat

Oh is it so bad?
Requesting a lobster bib
At the Harvester

Head like a pudding
Tummy full of pine needles
Boxing Day regret

Why the need to pee
The moment washing up starts?
Answer that, Brian Cox

A snackless wedding
The congregation hangry
All pray for divorce

The crushing pressure
Finding a pub quiz team name
Blank sheet stares at you

You point out again
Chips are a vegetable
It is your mantra

Are these deckchairs free?
The glower on the man's face
Indicates they're not

'CHEESE IS NOT PUDDING'
The restaurant goes quiet
You sit down again

I'm a little lost
It's only bread and butter
Why is it eight quid?

Ice lolly remnants
Dangle precariously
From the bejoked stick

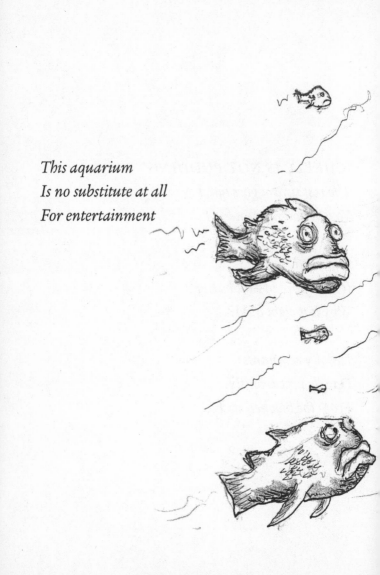

This aquarium
Is no substitute at all
For entertainment

The dog in this pub
Just stares into the distance
Must have seen some things

Caff's not yet open
You see them inside waiting
While you fail to eat

Holy fucking shit
Why is this film three hours long?
Nothing is that good

'Two pounds ninety-nine
For a bloody Solero?'
The sound of summer

Does this pub have crisps?
I cannot see any crisps
This pub must have crisps?

It is guaranteed
One filling will not arrive
In a caff omelette

I'm not full of faith
The youth running this waltzer
Will not let me die

No one seems happy
With a metal detector
Have they found themselves?

The trousers of youths
Why are they ridiculous
To all mature eyes?

The phrase 'wine o'clock'
Spoken or in tea-towel form
Has to be hate speech

Overheard phone call
No one wants to hear about
Your loft conversion

See an old schoolfriend
Have they achieved more than me?
No, thankfully not

Shorts are a bold choice
When your lower leg looks like
Cut-rate mac and cheese

I don't see the point
Of hearing your opinion
When you have that beard

Old man on the bus
Crisps with separate salt bag
Where did he get those?

The weather discussed
Health problems are reported
No more chat with aunt

You look down upon
All public urination
Except your own, obvs

Yes, you have a horn
I'm glad it gives you pleasure
Now put it away

Spider near my head
Feels like the size of a horse
Due to cowardice

You have bought your round
Empty glass sits before you
Nudge them with your mind

I see your backpack
Is one designed for a child
I can't be your friend

You are obnoxious
But you have a neck tattoo
So I will leave it

Could you stop talking
About your new allotment?
Your mangetout are shit

The perfect aunt gift
Otters on a calendar
Leave the shop smugly

'It's preposterous'
Huffs a ruddy man loudly
In the betting shop

A worrying sight
A man walking with a spade
When it is dark out

From your Instagram
It appears your life is great
But I know better

'So they call you Squits
How did you get that nickname?'
Ah yes, now I see

You have used 'methinks'
So you've lost the argument
Before it's started

You have mistaken
That lady for Bob Dylan
And now it's too late

Possession of a
Personalized number plate
Helps speed judgement up

Thighs clad in Lycra
Band T-shirt taut across gut
Mid-life crisis looms

Oh sweet Jesus, no
No, no, no, no, no, no, no
Not a hen party

Hungry in transit
Could I swipe that kid's Snickers
And blame that small dog?

You seem very proud
Of your expansive moustache
Though it's just lip hair

Your phone does not need
To bleep with each button push
You are inhumane

Should I tell that man
Or should he learn the hard way
About his trousers?

'It's warm in the sun'
Tell me something I don't know
Stupid old person

Lady on the bus
Should I offer her a seat?
You do and she cries

Your veganism
Is no substitute for a
Personality

I have to question
Why you are talking to me
When I don't know you

Your internet date
Barely recognizable
Thirty-one my arse

Your inclusion of
An errant apostrophe
Means we can't be friends

Deeply suspicious
Two adults on a tandem
Wearing matching shorts

So you're an expert?
But let us never forget
All wine tastes the same

'Have you been busy?'
And 'What time do you finish?'
Asked in every cab

Pork scratchings, plain crisps
Plus a large Bloody Mary
Makes a sort of roast

Food delivery
You have no change for a tip
Meat Feast tastes bitter

Ghost attacks likely
Changing a duvet cover
Like a ghost yourself

A sneeze emanates
Could this just be hayfever?
Or something fatal?

FLIMSY TISSUES
The Merest
Breeze Will
Breach them

Winner of the meat
Looks just like the ticket man
This raffle is fixed

It crosses your mind
During every taxi ride
That they'll murder you

Celebration time
Anniversary beckons
Wetherspoons again

Sniff the sausages
You examine their colour
'Best by' date elapsed

I have broken wind
It was not a cry for help
But an ill-timed egg

What excuse could work?
Getting out of a wedding
Cholera at least

Why would a grown man
Have a haircut of that kind?
You are a disgrace

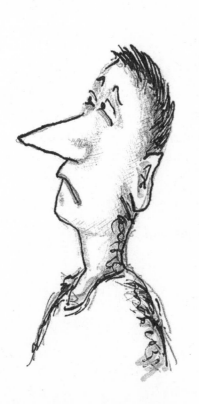

Now, wine before beer?
Or is it beer before wine?
Which one's the bad one?

There's no need to chat
Seated in the barber's chair
Or anywhere else

'Oh, is that the time?'
You hear yourself say out loud
What else could it be?

Drinking before nine
Should only really occur
Christmas and airports

Oh, words can wound you
Especially ones such as
Insufficient funds

Hospital visit
Are grapes still acceptable?
Or will I be mocked?

A simple question
'Have you a loyalty card?'
Disgust hits your face

It is ironic
Wearing a Union Jack hat
Proves you're not British

Mushy peas, gravy
Some dampness for my chips, please
I am from the North

How will all this end?
Automatic toilet door
Your fate in its hands

You ask earnestly
If I want some vegan cheese
Crusty silence falls

Budget samosa
Bought from dodgy corner shop
The taste of regret

This skateboarder seems
To be at least forty-two
It's a toy, you know

Don't draw attention
To the dagger in your flank
'Oh it's just a scratch'

The smell of dog mess
Search for the culprit begins
Soles solemnly checked

This is a chip shop
Why are your chips not ready?
You're not a wait shop

Why can't Monster Munch
Be offered as a starter?
Are you royalty?

At a christening
Smell of burnt eggs wafts the room
Blame it on the child

'Why am I sober?'
You say that phrase to yourself
A startling amount

'Can you watch my stuff?'
Instantly you're vigilant
Scanning for ram-raids

'Oh, you're the artist?'
Too late. You have already
Besmirched his daubings

How did we escape
Painful social intercourse
Before mobile phones?

What's the allowed time
Between waking and a nap?
Twelve minutes for me

You have been cut up
By a white Honda Accord
Vengeance will be swift

A sandwich for lunch
There are no other options
Mandated by law

Every roadworks
Features one hard-hatted man
Looking in the hole

Bus stop in the rain
You focus on the display
Praying for a sign

A correlation
Between the hardness of seat
And length of the play

Disabled parking
You eye the car there with doubt
'They'd better be blind'

Trying not to cry
At a terrible haircut
Still leave a tip though

Everything's improved
When presented in pie form
Yes, even divorce

'Don't point that at me'
Not the thing you want to hear
Romantically

Can I please propose
A new national anthem?
Countdown *theme's quite nice*

Why did I decide
To fry this bacon topless?
Fat spits on my nips

A child is crying
I should show some sympathy
But tutting more fun

Confused in London
Is that a trendy person?
Or sadly homeless?

It's cream and then jam
Or else it's jam and then cream
It's the sconely way

Fancy dress party
Your entrance makes quite a splash
Costume deemed hate crime

Self-service checkout
Items are not recognized
Unexpectedly

Is there a Shazam
To identify Revels?
That would be handy

'For shits and giggles'
or, put it another way
A waste of my time

There was no warning
Country dancing was involved
And now here we are

Florist confusion
'And what flowers would you like?'
'Nice ones that are cheap'

Scorn is evident
As you befriend the guide dog
And then see his sign

You said this meeting
Was absolutely vital
This was not the case